FUNNY BRUMMIE PICTURES

The Art of Robert Geoghegan

Robert Geoghegan

BREWIN BOOKS

BREWIN BOOKS
19 Enfield Ind. Estate,
Redditch,
Worcestershire,
B97 6BY
www.brewinbooks.com

Published by Brewin Books 2020

A CIP catalogue record for this book is
available from the British Library.

ISBN: 978-1-85858-724-0

Printed and bound in Great Britain by
Page Bros Ltd.

FUNNY BRUMMIE PICTURES

The Art of Robert Geoghegan

For Margaret

Introduction

I was always known as 'the artist' in my class at primary school and the person to go to when drawing something. I had a wonderfully eccentric teacher called Miss Luke who I remember painting a picture of Guy Fawkes night in front of the class and teaching us about Michelangelo drawing the perfect circle freehand in a competition for a papal commission. Unfortunately all this magic and mystery that pictures can bring got lost in the more prosaic academic system of my grammar school and it was the 1970s when abstract art held rein and being able to draw well didn't seem to impress my art teacher. So I made the ridiculous decision of choosing Geography at 'O' Level instead of Art – it was one or the other – as somehow this would look better for a university application? Madness, although I have nothing against Geography and was quite interested in it but drawing was my talent and it had been overlooked. Anyway, no 'O' level, no 'A' level and no on to an Art degree for me.

As well as Art, English was my other favourite subject. My dad was a great reader and had a bookcase full of novels in the house, he always took us to the library as children. So I eventually went on to do a degree in English and Library Studies. Once I graduated I knew I wanted to go back to my drawing and painting and so enrolled at Bournville Art College on several part-time courses. I did lots of life drawing because for some reason I knew I needed to be able to draw figures and people properly though I wasn't that sure why at the time. For some years I did drawings and writings in an illustrated diary form, of life in my parish primary schools and youth club. So already the drawing and writing combination was there. I was also beginning to write short humorous pieces, some as poems, others as prose, based on my observations of hum drum daily life like buying a Cornish pasty from a bakers or after overhearing a conversation on a bus about a work colleague who knew everything about stationery. My painting was separate to this. I was painting trees and flowers in the local parks. When I showed these I got some nice comments but nothing more. There was nothing very different about them I suppose.

Then in 2004 I had my epiphany moment. I was helping my sister out, looking after my little nephew and of course he wanted to walk on a wall instead of the pavement. I saw in my mind's eye an image of a mum on the wall with the shopping bags and the toddler on the street beckoning "Come on Mom!" I remember scribbling this down in a little notebook. When I eventually got round to doing the drawing using pen and watercolour I had Lidl as the supermarket which I changed to Pidl and so I was up and running. Now 16 years later I have about 170 images which mostly have

Robert's first Funny Brummie picture "Come on Mom!" produced in 2004.

a joke and caption in them and are based on my Birmingham surroundings – so Funny Brummie Pictures. Again it was that combination of picture and writing that I was drawn to. I would say the visual side dominates my time as some of the paintings can take me anything between 20 to 30 hours to complete. However I do take time on writing the accompanying caption many times until I'm happy with the wording.

So in 2004 I started producing these scenes of everyday life with a caption underneath them. They often involved some word play and puns. I began by working on A4 hot pressed – which is smooth – watercolour paper. This smooth surface allowed for detail and pen work. After completing about 20 or more I knew I wanted to get my ideas out and show them to people. These were the days before Instagram and Facebook which are my main social media platforms today. I knew they had an exhibition space in the Birmingham Central Library on the 3rd floor. I enquired and booked the space and put my work up. I remember being on the escalator and seeing someone standing in front of one of my pictures and being excited that they could hold someone's interest. I put out a comments book to gauge reaction and when I saw some of the positive encouraging responses: "I laughed out loud", "Lovely way to depict Birmingham's diversity. Great fun" – I knew I was on to something and that people would relate to and show an interest in this type of picture.

Looking back at my first attempts I realise my style has developed over the years. Early on the ideas might have been good but I was drawing the scene out in a generic way from memory resulting in quite a weak image. I remember a comment in the book saying "Weak drawing" and knew I had to improve by drawing from close observation. Over time and with the help of Google images and taking my own photographs, I was able to research the visual references I needed for each painting to make an authentic realistic portrayal of whatever I was representing. Now I'm able to look up particular expressions on people's faces to help me communicate what's happening in the picture as well as researching particular types of clothing and footwear for the characters in the paintings. My mantra has been local, funny and the best quality painting I can do. These three qualities working together make for a strong often saleable image.

Selling prints of these paintings and making a living from it along side my teaching art, I suppose has given me an endorsement that I'm doing something right though I know the art critics probably wouldn't see it like that but I'm interested in pleasing the public and not them. From the start my aim was to get as many Birmingham people as I could to buy one at least of my pictures. So to sell a lot at a reasonable price depending on size of print was my plan. Probably my highlight was selling 19 prints in one Sunday morning at the mac monthly Art Market to Simon who used to be in the youth club I helped at and then he emailed to say he wanted 4 more to put all together on his bathroom wall. It's great when I know people have collections of my pictures. Anyway I knew private galleries were not for me – not enough people enter them and pricing is prohibitive but art and craft markets would be. So for nearly 15 years I have sold my pictures at Moseley Art Market and at all sorts of other venues across the city – the mac, All Saints Square in Kings Heath, Highbury Hall, Harborne Carnival, school fetes, open garden

Robert displaying his work at Artsfest, Birmingham in 2010.

Robert's stall at Birmingham Christmas Craft Market in 2015.

weekends, local history fairs, Sarehole Mill, The Barber Institute, St Philip's Cathedral Square, even House of Fraser! You name somewhere in Birmingham and I'm likely to have had a stall there and of course at the five week Birmingham Christmas Craft Market on Broad Street in the good old days before Centenary Square development and demolition of the Central Library. One Saturday in December I remember selling 55 pictures in the one day – my record to date. All this is about reaching as many people as I can with my pictures. I like it when people come across my work and they say "Oh I've seen these in other people's houses." The markets, as well as a place to make some money, are a great way to meet the people of Birmingham and I get all sorts of different stories and responses to my pictures with people giving their own slant on a place, fad or an event. They are the people who encourage me to keep coming up with new ideas and paintings.

So not for me the struggling 'Oh he never sold anything in his lifetime so he must be a genius'. I produce the pictures with the people of Birmingham and those who have left the city in mind. That's my audience and I always think after meeting and chatting with them on my stalls that when I work on a picture I do it as well as I can as they deserve something well done about their city. I remember attending a talk by the artist and sculptor Raymond Mason, back in the 1980s, at the Birmingham Museum and Art Gallery. Born in Birmingham he made representational sculpture about a well loved Paris fruit market before it was swept away by modern development and one showing the aftermath of a mining disaster. He described wanting to give his audience 'a full meal' and that really resonated with me. A bit of local pride I suppose even if sometimes it's a funny take on the amazing variety of subject matter that we have here in Birmingham. Growing up in the 1970s I felt very alienated by my home city. How could I do art about this place? I should be in London, or New York or the Lake District. Always somewhere else. Only much later by reading up about Birmingham's history and knowing stories behind local places did I realise that I could give meaning and significance to what can appear initially quite mundane and everyday. So a big thing for me is look at what's on your own doorstep. You'll be surprised how interesting it can be if you take a bit of time to look and think about it.

The pictures in this book are not arranged in any particular order but obviously I have my favourite themes and the city buses are probably what I'm best known for. Never having driven myself, I've been driven about by Birmingham buses all my life and I suppose I began getting ideas to feature them in my paintings from the destination names: Druids Heath, Maypole, Bearwood, Outer and Inner Circle. The fact that when I started and until quite recently the buses were a lovely striking red colour was great for me visually as the pictures would catch the eyes of passers by on my stalls especially in large poster size. I'm able to people the bus with any character I like from the Queen and Prince Philip to Lou Reed and Hattie Jacques. I've had the drivers as druids, paramedics, Father Christmas, bears, Marlon Brando, an astronaut and Stevie Wonder which probably wouldn't be a good idea. I've been able to change the number plates to the unique postcode of Buckingham Palace or the date of the summer solstice and transform the window wipers into crutches and even picture a bus on the wrong side of the road. People at my stalls often ask me have I done a picture of a particular bus number but sadly if the destination yields no visual pun then the answer will be no. I feel as if I've nearly exhausted this particular seam but still would like to do one on the number 2 bus to Gospel Oak.

Another of my interests beside Birmingham buses are Birmingham buildings from the modern – I think I've done about four versions of Selfridges through to the Victorian with the Law Courts right back to the Jacobean with Aston Hall and I think the oldest would have to be The Old Crown in Digbeth. Then there's the city's football teams – Blues, Villa and West Brom. Of course on my stalls this always causes a bit of fun when a Blues fan has to flick through the Villa pictures and I remember once on my card stand all the Blues cards had been turned round with their backs showing.

I've tried to choose a varied cross section to include in this volume but it is a selection and only about a third of the total. I have done lots of pictures about where I live – so of Moseley and Kings Heath which I thought wouldn't have such a city wide interest and so many of these are omitted. It was difficult to know what to put in and what to leave out but I think it is a good representation of my work. And I haven't finished yet!

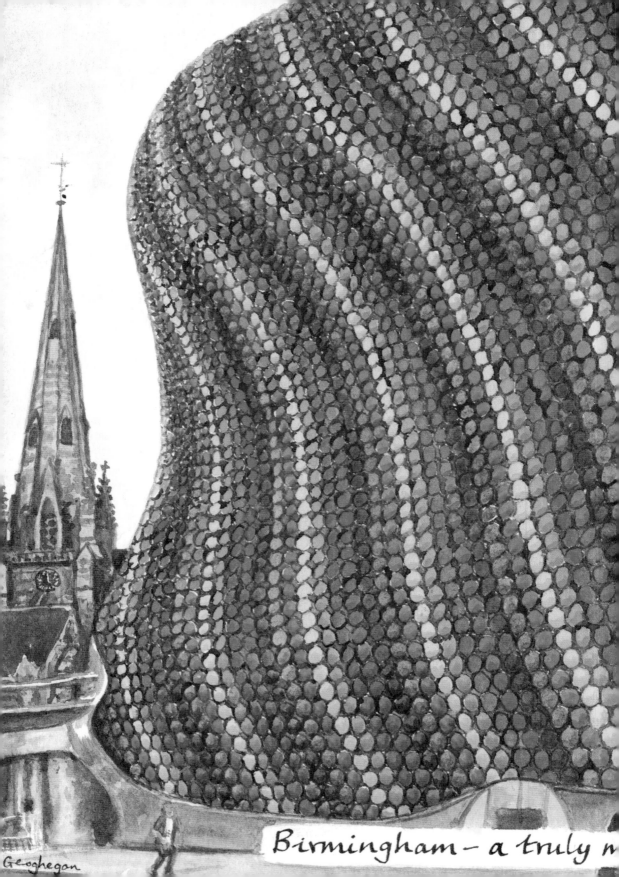

Birmingham — a truly m

Geoghegan

lticolourful city.

▲ Thomas Attwood Statue (2009 watercolour)

People always said about this popular public sculpture that it looked like a real person sitting on the steps near the Town Hall and these police obviously think he's up to no good as I should think this is an Alcohol Restricted Zone. Thomas Attwood was a Birmingham MP who lobbied Parliament for Electoral reform in the first half of the 19th Century.

▶ There's going to be a fight (2012 oil)

Here Birmingham's Iron Man sculpture is squaring up to a rather oversized Cyberman from Dr Who. The caption: "There's going to be a fight" I remembered from a Laurel and Hardy film where the crowd gets bigger and bigger as the word gets out. Remember school fights in the playground?

"There's going to be a fight."

R Geoghegan

"Tickets and passes please. If all's correct then no one gets hurt."

▲ Ticket Inspection   (2014 oil)

"Tickets and passes please. If all's correct then no one gets hurt."

The appearance of the ticket inspectors on the bus usually draws a sharp intake of breath and here they have back up in the form of Tommy and Arthur Shelby of the Peaky Blinders. Luckily my bus pass was valid that day.

▶ The Posh Bus   (2013 oil)

"Sorry duck – no more pushchairs."

I can't claim this one was completely my idea as a young woman at Moseley Art Market looking at my pictures asked if I would do one about the Number 1 bus – 'The Posh Bus' as she called it. She said she worked in Five Ways and everyone on it at a certain time in the morning looked nice and 'posh' going into their office jobs. I must say I was pleased with my 'Upstairs Downstairs' reference with the toffs from Downton Abbey upstairs and the cooks downstairs. Downton's chauffeur Tom Branson is the bus driver and the Queen and Prince Philip are making use of their senior citizens bus passes.

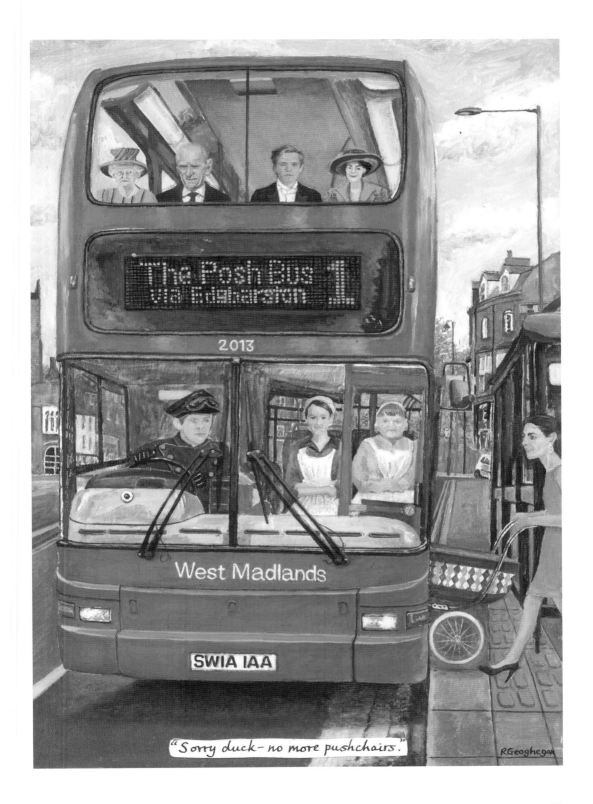

I do enjoy watching the bus drivers engaging in friendly banter.

That Jasper Carrott sketch still has repercussions as to where people position themselves on Birmingham buses to this day.

▲ **Jasper Carrott Sketch**   (2017 oil)

'That Jasper Carrott sketch still has repercussions as to where passengers position themselves on Birmingham buses to this day.'

Would you believe it I did this picture well before the first murmurings of Corona virus. I've used the Birmingham buses all my life but I'm sure over, say, the last ten years passengers have become more antisocial and have the infuriating habit of blocking the inside seat. Then I began to think of that old 1970s 'Nutter on the bus' sketch by Jasper Carrott – you probably wouldn't get away with that today – which would give them some justification possibly for this 'social distancing'. We've all been there though haven't we if you're a bus user. I always think it makes the bus journey more interesting?

◀ **Bus Driver Banter**   (2017 oil)

'I do enjoy watching the bus drivers engaging in friendly banter.'

I'm not sure if it's possible to arm wrestle without a table top but these two are having a go.

Getting down with the kids.

▲ **Lollipop Man**   (2011 oil)

'Getting down with the kids.'

There can't be many jobs where you get to dress so brightly. I had this idea when getting the bus up to Kings Heath with the school day starting and the friendly lollipop man was high fiving the Queensbridge students as they crossed the road to school.

▶ **Birmingham Mail Kiosk**   (2011 oil)

"You're looking a bit down today Ted. Anything the matter?"

I'm not sure when exactly these kiosks disappeared from the city centre but it was inevitable with the drop of physical newspaper sales due to online platforms. In 2011 I had fun selecting the grimmest headlines I could find but the ones about the City Binmen Strike and even more so about the Swine Flu spread are a bit too prescient.

"You're looking a bit down today Ted. Anything the matter?"

R Geoghegan

9·29 am and some poor sod attempting to use his Off Peak Bus Pass. R.Geoghegan

▲ **Off Peak Bus Pass**   (2008 watercolour)

"Exterminate! Exterminate!"

'9.29 am and some poor sod attempting to use his Off Peak Bus Pass.'

I did this picture from bitter experience as I've been there as a 'twearly' though thankfully I've upgraded to a full pass now so don't have to be desperately checking the time just before 9.30 am. I like to get the odd Dr Who reference into some of my pictures hence the Dalek bin and the Cyberman passenger. By the way this is my bus stop outside Fivelands Vets for the 50 bus up to Kings Heath and Asda – other supermarkets are available.

◀ **Platinum Bus**   (2016 oil)

'So slick they're bringing in Cybermen to drive them.'

Peter Crouch: "Extra leg room? Let me be the judge of that."

I was a bit alarmed when some years ago West Midlands Travel started to bring in these more energy efficient platinum buses which are grey as I really liked painting the red ones. However this is the trend and the red buses are being phased out. West Mondas? – Mondas is the planet the Cybermen are from.

▲ Aston Hall by Torchlight (2010 watercolour)

"For God's sake – move it! … the cops are 'ere."

Remember Aston Hall by Candlelight? I don't think they have it any more. I remember going a couple of times. They held it in November and I remember feeling awkward with people dressed up in Tudor costume role playing, addressing the public with 'thee' and 'thou' which encouraged you to make a quick exit to the next room. It did look pretty though candlelit. As for my picture I'm not sure what the climbing burglar has to hang on to – maybe it's a Brummie Spiderman?

▶ The Barton Arms (2017 oil)

"Well here's another fine mess you've gotten us into!"

(Arthur Stanley Jefferson and Norvell Hardy stayed here while performing at the Aston Hippodrome opposite).

This beautiful historical building is also a pre-match drinking pub for Villa fans so here Stan and Laurel have definitely picked the wrong Birmingham team to support.

"Well here's another fine mess you've gotten us into!"
(Arthur Stanley Jefferson and Norvell Hardy stayed here
while performing at the Aston Hippodrome opposite).

R Geoghegan

Nice to see a bus driver so willing to assist with directions.

Partially sighted dalek.

▲ **Partially Sighted Dalek**   (2011 oil)

I enjoyed painting this dalek with its cool combination of silver, gold and blues. The picture has High Street Birmingham as its setting with M&S in view. This particular painting is special to me as it was the first one I painted in oils after producing them for the previous seven years in watercolour, at the time it seemed quite a big deal to change my medium. Oils have allowed me to make many changes to my compositions as I go along and also paint figures etc on top of backgrounds I paint in first.

◀ **Five Ways Bus Driver**   (2019 oil)

'Nice to see a bus driver so willing to assist with directions.'

This is definitely the first time I've drawn someone with five arms – two is normally difficult enough. I suppose now I don't need to ask the driver when to get off as I rarely travel to a new part of Birmingham where I've not been before. I know some drivers are helpful, others less so but I think the separating screen on the National Express buses doesn't help 'friendly' interaction between driver and passenger.

Less than a month into his year as Lord Mayor and yet another civic engagement not quite going according to plan.

▲ Civic Engagement (2009 watercolour)

'Less than a month into his year as Lord Mayor and yet another civic engagement not quite going according to plan.'

Although Bullie's always being dressed up in cute and fitting outfits at different times throughout the year, I'm always amazed at how angry his expression is when you study it. Here is a flight of fancy with Birmingham's Lord Mayor being tossed by Bullie to the horror of the surrounding dignitaries and school children with their certificates.

▶ King Kong Outside Council House (2011 oil)

"He's back!"

For a while there was a bit of a campaign to try to bring back to Birmingham the King Kong statue that graced Manzoni Gardens in the 'new' Bullring briefly in 1972-73. If that were to happen where would he be positioned? I thought Birmingham City Council House would be a really prominent site for him but the shocked Lord Mayor at the window doesn't seem so keen.

"Sorry - no Irish".

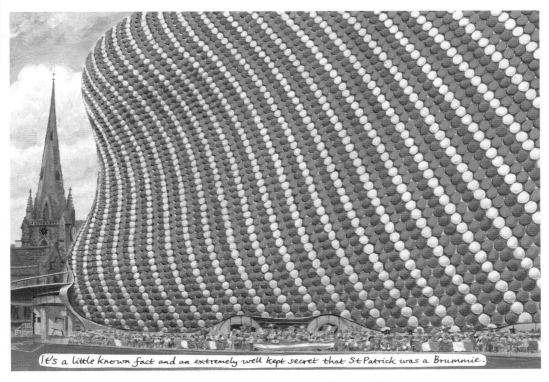

It's a little known fact and an extremely well kept secret that St Patrick was a Brummie.

▲ **Selfridges, Bullring on St Patrick's Day Parade** (2014 oil)

'It's a little known fact and an extremely well kept secret that St Patrick was a Brummie.'

Another of my versions of the Selfridges building Bullring, only this time getting an Irish make over. I think they do light it up an eerie green at night over St Patrick's week – 'week' which means the local Digbeth pubs can stretch the celebrations out over seven days. It is a worry when people read the caption on this picture and ask me "Was he really a Brummie?"

◄ **O'Neill's, Moseley** (2012 oil)

"Sorry – no Irish."

My dad had Irish grandparents and my mum was Irish and I've been visiting where she grew up all my life. With these justifications out of the way this picture is funny: wearing the green and being stopped entry to an Irish pub on St Patrick's Day / Night is just daft but serious: with the notices in the 1950s placed by landlords in renting accommodation throughout England. O'Neill's is no longer in Moseley, changing to The One Trick Pony in 2014.

When Dracula and his brides visit Birmingham, they stay here at Holy Trinity church, Bordesley and on this particular occasion, enjoyed perfect weather.

▲ Dracula's Birmingham Abode (2016 oil)

'When Dracula and his brides visit Birmingham, they stay here at Holy Trinity church, Bordesley and on this particular occasion, enjoyed perfect weather.'

I remember having great fun working on this one. This gothic structure is sadly fenced off now but has that scary look about it that inspired me to have Dracula and his brides staying there overnight. I have been inside there about 30 years ago when I briefly volunteered to run art sessions there when it was being used as a centre for homeless men.

▶ Goths in Pigeon Park (2008 watercolour)

I remember enjoying researching this one to get some classic goth looks which tend to involve a lot of black clothing and a lot of white make up. The grounds around St Philip's Cathedral in the city centre has gravestones and slabs dotted around so it was a perfect place for flocks of goths to congregate. They were always good humoured, often high spirited though some people frowned that they were sitting on tombs and made big bare patches on the grass. Anyway in this picture they have got their comeuppance. The question is where have they all gone as you no longer see them here today. Maybe the craze / tribe has died out – pardon the pun or they have relocated to a graveyard near you.

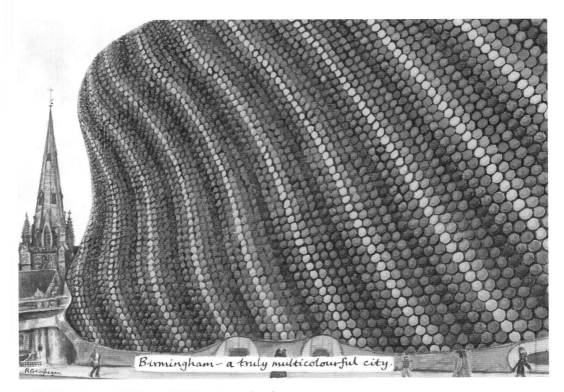

Birmingham – a truly multicolourful city.

▲ **Multi-colourful City** (2009 watercolour)

'Birmingham – a truly multi-colourful city.'

When people see this picture they think of Gay Pride but to be honest I did it well before I even knew the rainbow was its symbol though I know I can be a bit behind the curve sometimes. Changing multi-cultural to multi-colourful gave me licence to alter the grey, silver discs to bright colours. It looks like rainbow colours but I've added pink just for good measure. It took me ages of course to finish this one but it was quite satisfying filling them all in having made sure I'd got the repeat colour order correct. Some people say they wish the real Selfridges was coloured like that but I think that might be a bit hard on the eyes especially on that scale.

◀ **Bullie looking mad!** (2010 watercolour)

'Jumped and sat on by snotty nosed kids, flashbulbs continually going off in your face, chainstore window fronts as your only view, periodically scratched and pooped on from high, sold as a postcard in city centre newskiosks – wouldn't you be mad?'

'Once a mod, always a mod.'

▲ **Mobility Scooter Mod** (2010 watercolour)

'Once a mod, always a mod.'

After looking through lots of photographs of mods with their scooters, parkas, target signs and flags I came up with this cool old guy proudly zooming down Silver Street in Kings Heath after doing a bit of shopping at Lidl. The two school girls look well impressed. My mum lived in one of those 'warden controlled' flats for over fifteen years even though there wasn't a warden there for most of that time.

▶ **Trainee Bus Driver** (2015 oil)

"This guy's a natural."

I really did my homework for this one. I'd occasionally seen these white buses – usually single decker – for training bus drivers on the road but hadn't been able to get a photograph of one stationary. So I contacted West Midland Travel / National Express and they kindly arranged for me to meet up with one of their instructors at the Walsall Bus Depot. This instructor was immaculately dressed even in his hi vis jacket and told me he took great pride in maintaining high standards so he'd be horrified to see the picture I came up with which I decided not to send on to them as I'm not sure how they'd react. By the way the setting for this one is Kings Heath High Street.

"Excuse me please – do you have the correct time?
And could you please direct me to the Jewellery Quarter."
"You stupid...stupid boy."

"A little bit of cloud cover and the daft buggers don't show."

▲ **Soho House, Handsworth** (2013 oil)

"A little bit of cloud cover and the daft buggers don't show."

I've pictured the great man himself Matthew Boulton outside his swanky mansion Soho House in Handsworth getting very frustrated that his mates from the Lunar Society have not showed up simply because the moon isn't bright enough to light the way.

◀ **The Chamberlain Clock, Birmingham Jewellery Quarter** (2014 oil)

Youth: "Excuse me please – do you have the correct time? And could you please direct me to the Jewellery Quarter."

Police: "You stupid … stupid boy."

I remember that painting this impressive ornate clock was not easy with all its panelling and gilded decoration. I tried to make the young lad's attire generic: hoodie, chinos and vans.

'There's nothing new under the sun.'

R Geoghegan

▲ Birmingham Trams Old and New (2016 oil)

'There's nothing new under the sun.'

I've pictured this one near the bottom of Corporation Street so I could get the New Look shop in. The last double decker tram to run in Birmingham was back in 1953 and now things have come full circle with the re-introduction of trams in the city centre after over a 60 year absence in 2015. I liked the original pink and silver livery but the fleet have changed to blue now.

▶ Maypole 50 Bus (2010 watercolour)

This was my second bus painting after 'Druids' bus' and for a long time was my most popular selling print. Over the years I bet a lot of bus drivers have felt like the one pictured here, having to deal with worse things than a bunch ('troupe'?) of Morris Dancers boarding their vehicle. The Fighting Cocks pub has had a name change.

Just as exhilarating, Just as scary!

R Geoghegan.

Oh those happy carefree days before those three words 'Health and Safety' reared their silly head.

▲ **Birmingham Corporation Bus** (2013 oil)

'Oh those happy carefree days before those three words "Health and Safety" reared their silly head.'

Here's a bit of nostalgia as those of us of a certain age can remember jumping on and off these open back buses which I think were withdrawn in the mid 1970s. I'm not sure if you'd want your children having this much fun on the back of the bus especially with that motorbike in pursuit. I like the cream and navy livery on them. This picture hasn't a definite setting as I worked from an old black and white photograph of Co-operative shop fronts which had no location on it. Definitely more care free days but I'm sure more accident filled days as well, especially in the work place.

◀ **Shaky Bus ride** (2008 watercolour)

'Just as exhilarating, just as scary!'

There was a time when they had these televisions on buses mostly showing ads I think but I remember seeing white water rafting on such a screen and making the link of how you can be tossed about equally when getting up to get off the bus.

Commuters hurrying for their trains and praying:
'Please, please let it be the right sort of snow.'

R.Geoghegan

▲ Birmingham Snow Hill Station (2014 oil)

'Commuters hurrying for their trains and praying: "Please, please let it be the right sort of snow".'

This picture was fun to do with the neon lights and snow falling and lots of back views to paint in.

▶ Number 11 Bus Stop (2009 watercolour)

This painting was done from bitter experience of waiting for the famous but also infamous number 11 which is notorious for coming in threes after a half hour wait. The stop shown is at the top of Vicarage Road (I've stood there) Kings Heath and there is no sign of a bus on the horizon.

▲ **Viking Week**   (2019 oil)

"I know they used to have something called the Tulip Festival down here years ago but no one ever mentioned anything about 'Viking Week'."

I knew when I first saw the new swan pedalos on Cannon Hill Park lake I would have to do a picture featuring them. Over recent years I've taught children in schools how to make a Viking Longship model so it was nice to be able to put one into one of my Funny Brummie pictures.

By the way there isn't really a Viking Week in Cannon Hill Park but it might be a good idea?

Weoley Castle (on a good day)

RGeoghegan

▲ Weoley Castle (on a good day) (2017 oil)

If any one heads over to Weoley Castle in south Birmingham expecting to see a fortress with a moat and flags fluttering from the turrets they will be sorely disappointed. In reality all that remains is a bit of a wall and lots of grass. However, there is a Weoley Castle Historical Society which put on occasional re-enactments. I think I might have got a bit carried away in the picture with burning pitch being poured from the battlements.

Somehow she always seemed capable of finding the positive in every situation.

D ogs , dogs ... and more flippin' dogs.

R Geoghegan

▲ **Dog Woman**   (2010 watercolour)

'Dogs, dogs … and more flippin' dogs.'

I remember seeing someone wearing this doggie fleece and thinking – that deserves a picture.

I went to a shop in the Rag Market where they sell them and took a couple of photos of the fleece as you do. The setting for the picture is Highbury Road, Kings Heath which as you see is very long. Of course this is near Kings Heath and Highbury Parks – the latter especially a dog walker's heaven. Then it was a matter of researching a variety of dog breeds to make it interesting and of course one of the jokes here is the owner looks like one of the dogs. I think there's a law now that you can only walk three at a time so dog woman is totally disregarding that.

◀ **Interesting Font**   (2008 watercolour)

'Somehow she always seemed capable of finding the positive in every situation.'

"Interesting font they're now using on these new bus timetables."

I know I went through a phase of being obsessed by graffiti on bus shelters, and this painting manifests this. It was enjoyable trying to copy the free flourishes of the 'tags' and I might have added one or two for effect. I was pleased with the way the rain drops on the glass turned out.

▲ Santa Bus Driver (2012 oil)

On this Christmassy bus picture I went a bit over the top with the boarding passengers dressed in their winter woollies and sporting their reindeer hats. My first idea was to have Santa as a grumpy driver with the passengers being all jolly and festive but I removed the caption as I've used the painting as a Christmas card so I didn't want a negative mood on it.

▲ **Santa Tram Driver** (2017 oil)

'A hi tech Santa moving with the times.'

Another of my Birmingham Christmas pictures which I sell as a Christmas card. I've definitely used a bit of artistic license here with the track as coming down Corporation Street the tram should be on the right hand side and I've added a pleasing curve rather than straight track. Some paintings I really enjoy working on and I remember this was one.

"Now please, please! this year dear... promise me you won't mention it".

▲ **The Birmingham Frankfurt Christmas Market** (2009 watercolour)

"Now *please, please*! This year dear... promise me you won't mention it."

Everyone knows 'Fawlty Towers' don't they?

▶ **Santa Iron Man** (2009 watercolour)

I've done several paintings featuring the Iron Man. Personally I always think when Antony Gormley is interviewed – the creator of this work, he always comes over as a bit pompous and too high brow for me so putting a santa hat on one of his works was quite satisfying. This image always sells well as a Christmas card.

R Geoghegan.

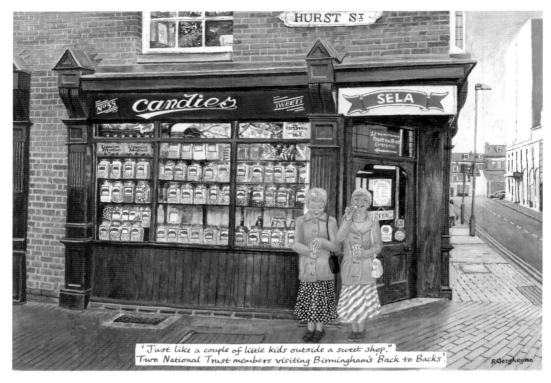

'Just like a couple of little kids outside a sweet shop.'
Two National Trust members visiting Birmingham's 'Back to Backs'.
R.Geoghegan

▲ Sweet Shop at Birmingham's Back to Backs (2014 oil)

'Just like a couple of little kids outside a sweet shop.'

Two National Trust members visiting Birmingham's Back to Backs.

What does a National Trust member look like? Well I came up with these two mature women who look like good friends who like to visit interesting places together. There's a little pun on one of the skirts which you may have spotted – patterned like the old sweets or the paper bag though most were probably just brown. Painting in all the glass jars of sweets was fun and I remember buying in a 000 size brush especially for this. Never again.

▲ **Outside Loos at Birmingham's Back to Backs** (2015 oil)

National Trust guided tour of Birmingham's Back to Backs.

"Incredible to think isn't it that our parents and our parents' parents struggled long and hard to escape from these conditions and here we are being asked to pay good money to view them?"

"Yes and she'll be asking us if we want to use them next."

My second Birmingham Back to Backs picture and pink tops seem to be popular on this particular tour. I've been twice on the tour and I would highly recommend it. Someone after seeing my picture remembered thinking while on the tour that the toilets were too clean and didn't pong enough but I'm not sure how much authenticity we really want when it comes to sanitary matters.

'Storm Joe is set to hit later with gusts of 100mph predicted in some parts of South Birmingham'.

'On March 15th 1903 there was a serious fire at the factory which is when hot chocolate made its first appearance' (extract from 'A History of Cadbury's, Bournville' by Errol Bean)

▲ Cadbury's Hot Chocolate (2018 oil)

'On March 15th 1903 there was a serious fire at the factory which is when hot chocolate made its first appearance' (Extract from 'A History of Cadbury's, Bournville' by Errol Bean)

One of my first Funny Brummie pictures where I haven't used colour but monochrome – all in burnt umber to be precise – as it's set in the past and I wanted to give it that sepia look and co-incidentally it's chocolate coloured as well. On my art stalls some people ask me "Is this true? Did it really happen" – no it's a joke. The fictional author Errol Bean gives a nod to the lead singer of the 70s pop group Hot Chocolate. I remember enjoying researching photos of old fire engines while working on this one – not sure how secure those ladders are?

◄ Storm Joe (2019 oil)

'Storm Joe is set to hit later with gusts of 100 mph predicted in some parts of South Birmingham.'

This picture presented me with the challenge of bending what is normally a very straight structure. These storms of course all have names now so why not Storm Joe for the Joseph Chamberlain University clocktower.

It's my one and only painting of a windy… extremely windy day.

'Keeping The Faith'.

R.Geoghegan

▲ **Keeping The Faith** (2014 oil)

That's all you can do when you're a Blues fan. It must be near the end of the season as there's a dad with his kids biting his nails – relegation threatens once again.

▶ **Stairway to Heaven (when we win)** (2019 oil)

This is one of my more positive Aston Villa pictures showing the fans expectantly climbing the steps of the Holte End to hopefully watch their team win (I so dislike painting steps – they're so difficult with the perspective and shading).

'Stairway to Heaven' (when we win).

R.Geoghegan

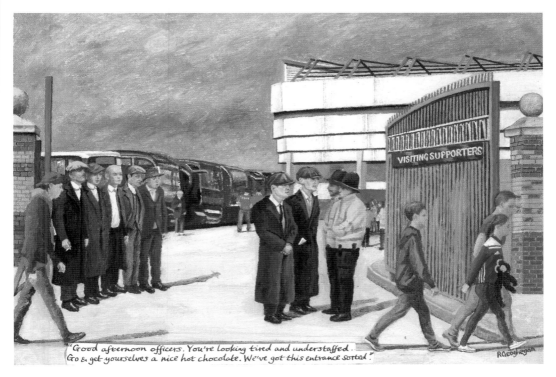

"Good afternoon officers. You're looking tired and understaffed. Go & get yourselves a nice hot chocolate. We've got this entrance sorted."

▲ **St Andrew's Match Day Policing**   (2018 oil)

Tommy Shelby: "Good afternoon officers. You're looking tired and understaffed. Go and get yourselves a nice hot chocolate. We've got this entrance sorted."

I quite like bringing the Peaky Blinders into modern times and here they're kindly offering their security services to a much stretched West Midlands Police Force. Due to the tribal nature of football this coach park area for the away supporters always has a high police presence on this gate.

◀ **Est. 1894 AVFC**   (2016 oil)

"If only they awarded points for tradition."

If you could see their faces – especially the granddad – they would be looking wistful and thinking back to the Glory Days of yore. Thanks to my nephew Cormac for modelling for the young lad in the painting. He is a Villa fan by the way.

▲ Proper Police   (2013 oil)

Have you noticed nowadays how many people are wearing hi vis jackets? Well here's three public servants going about their duties. I remember being especially taken with the striking bright yellow and purple jacket of the Colmore Business District street warden patrolling 'Pigeon Park' and this inspired me to do the painting. Sorry to all the PCSO's who I know do an important job.

▶ St Martin's and Selfridges   (2009 watercolour)

'The old, the new. Discuss.' I'd rather not.

It's a really interesting juxtaposition of these two buildings and is very Birmingham with the fairly old up against the new. Remember those type of exam questions where they gave you a quote and then 'Discuss'. Strange as I always thought a discussion was a two or more way dialogue where as here you were on your own with your pen and were just scrawling away for forty minutes.

'The old, the new. Discuss'
I'd rather not.

Such a beautiful ornate facade —
shame about the people.

R Geoghegan

Birmingham Central Library 1974-2013.
Architecturally, it may have been an 'inverted ziggurat' and inspired by the great standing Mayan temples built over two thousand years ago but not even the Jehovah Witnesses could save it from being 'knocked' after just forty years.

RGeoghegan

▲ Birmingham Central Library 1974-2013 (2015 oil)

'Architecturally it may have been an "inverted ziggurat" and inspired by the great standing Mayan temples built over two thousand years ago but not even the Jehovah Witnesses could save it from being "knocked" after just forty years.'

This is one of three paintings I've done of the no longer with us Birmingham Central Library – a view from the back. The Jehovah Witnesses stand to the right with their literature stand. I was sorry to see it go as I spent many hours studying for my 'A' levels and degree in its quiet, spacious reference area and just generally used it to borrow lots of books, music and audio books over the years. Some one who worked there recently told me that they have a piece of it – a concrete block – at home as a memento.

◀ Birmingham Victoria Law Courts (2013 oil)

'Such a beautiful ornate facade – shame about the people.'

I wouldn't normally go up to this part of town but the art materials store Spectrum moved there so I was passing this splendid building quite often. I remember this painting took me many hours work putting in all the detailed architectural decoration. I had fun with the people outside. A bit of an exaggeration but not too much.

The Beatles made their Birmingham debut here on York Rd, Kings Heath on 15th February 1963.

R.Geoghegan

▲ **The Ritz Ballroom, Kings Heath** (2015 oil)

'The Beatles made their Birmingham debut here on York Rd, Kings Heath on 15th February 1963.'

Here's a bit of Birmingham 60s nostalgia. The only photographs I could find of the Ballroom were black and white. I have memories of when it was a bingo hall and of this red and yellow colouring. This building began as a cinema, then a ballroom, then bingo hall and lastly a Cash Converters before sadly it burnt down. So many bands from the 60s played there, such as the Rolling Stones, the Kinks, the Moody Blues and Pink Floyd, that there has been a campaign to build a centre to celebrate its rich musical history.

▶ **The Anchor Pub, Digbeth** (2017 oil)

'I like this Birmingham by the Sea maritime pub tucked away in the back streets of salty Digbeth.'

You can imagine places like Portsmouth and Plymouth having lots of these maritime named pubs but inland Birmingham? I enjoyed putting in the press ganging, the old sea captain and of course the fishermen in their yellow oilskins.

I like this Birmingham by the Sea maritime pub tucked away in the back streets of salty Digbeth. R.Geoghegan

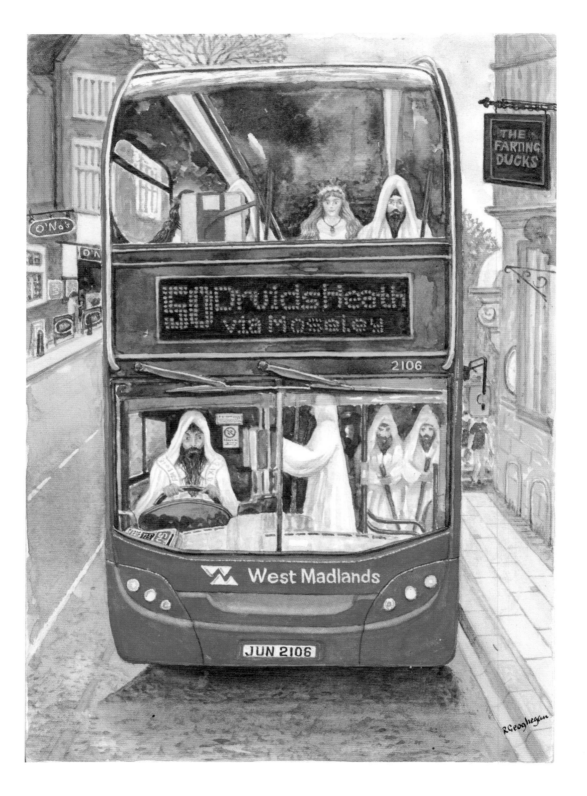

Police statement: "We judged it was in the public interest."
The Public: "He was asking for it."

R Geoghegan

▲ **Bad Busker** (2015 oil)

Police statement: "We judged it was in the public interest."
The Public: "He was asking for it."

I've set this picture on Birmingham New Street where most of the buskers set up. Personally I like them as they bring life and character to the city streets. I suppose if you worked in one of the premises nearby you are a bit exposed and can't escape but if they are really bad they tend to do fairly short stints and then move on. I got the idea for this one when tasers as a police tool had just been introduced and there's always something in the news about what's 'in the public interest'. The guy I've made up is probably doing another dreadful rendition of 'Wonderwall'.

◀ **Druids' Bus** (2008 watercolour)

This was my very first Birmingham bus picture which I painted back in 2008. For years Druids Heath was a place that I always thought had a certain ring to it and so one day I had the bright idea of picturing druids heading home on this bus route. Here the 50 bus is going through Moseley with The Fighting Cocks getting a name change. The number plate of the bus is the summer solstice date. I suppose now I'm best known for my bus pictures which to date I've done 26 and counting so I am forever grateful to Druids Heath for getting me started.

Of all the cities in the world, it would have to happen here, wouldn't it?

▲ **Alien Attack**   (2010 watercolour)

'Of all the cities in the world, it would have to happen here wouldn't it?'

The Birmingham Selfridges building has been called many things – a huge peanut, a blob, a giant metallic boob… but here I've turned it into an invading space craft. I've invented my own aliens who are zapping the poor shoppers. I enjoyed using purple, pink and a lurid green as the deadly beams of light.

▶ **A Short Hop**   (2018 oil)

"A short hop fare please driver."

The old ones are best. For people who aren't familiar with using buses, a 'short hop' is a fare which gets you about 2 stops.

I know there's some extremely bright people around here but...?

▲ **Astle Gates**   (2014 oil)

'Legend' in the true sense of the word.

This is my first of three West Brom pictures I've done and by far the most popular. When I started selling prints of my pictures at art markets in Birmingham I was surprised how many Baggies fans there are in this city as I kept being asked where's the West Brom picture as I already had several Blues and Villa ones on show. I put many hours work into painting this because of the fine elaborate wrought ironwork on the gates. I also made a false start, painting the gates nearly black from a poor colour photograph and so having to paint over what I'd done – very annoying.

The captions reads: "'Legend' in the true sense of the word", as players now play for a couple of seasons and become a club 'legend' whereas Jeff Astle scored 174 goals in 361 games for West Brom over ten years.

◄ **Old Joe**   (2009 watercolour)

'I know there's some extremely bright people around here but...?'

This was the first of several paintings I've done of the Chamberlain Clock Tower at Birmingham University in Edgbaston. This picture has one of my subtler jokes with the male student pointing at his wrist and asking the time with the massive clock looking down at him.

How on earth has a building as old as this survived so close to the centre of Birmingham! P.Geoghegan

▲ **The Old Crown, Digbeth**   (2017 oil)

'How on earth has a building as old as this survived so close to the centre of Birmingham?'

I always think this timber framed building from the 14th century, which in Lichfield or say Tewkesbury wouldn't look out of place, looks incongruous so near to the city centre of Birmingham. The joke therefore is that somehow it hasn't been demolished with the continuous construction work – hence the JCB diggers and men in hard hats and hi vis jackets – that has been going on in the city centre for the past fifty years and more.

▶ **Father Ted outside Cannon Hill Park Tearooms**   (2017 oil)

"Ah go on, go on, go on. Are you sure you won't have one Father? Go on, go on, go on."

I was quite pleased with three out of four of the likenesses in this painting but I seem to have enlarged Father Dougal's head. Never mind – they're recognisable I think. I've always worried about that large ceramic teapot hanging outside the Tearooms and that it is properly secured – here for Mrs Doyle's sake.

"Ah go on, go on, go on. Are you sure you won't have one Father? Go on, go on, go on".

R Geoghegan

73

Broad Street and Birmingham's 'Walk of Fame'.
"Never heard of 'im".
"That's probably because you're looking at a manhole cover."

R Geoghegan

When the planting up of this road island was complete, all that was required was this small finishing touch.

RCreaghegan

▲ **Road Traffic Island**   (2009 watercolour)

'When the planting up of this road island was complete, all that was required was this small finishing touch.'

With the recent warmer climate these fern trees have become more common in urban landscaping. This traffic island is where Salisbury, Russell, Willows and Edgbaston Roads meet beside Cannon Hill Park. Sorry – the dinosaur is a only flight of my imagination so you won't see it if you pass this way. Thank you to my nephew Joe for his model dinosaur that modelled for me for this painting.

◀ **Broad Street and Birmingham's 'Walk of Fame'**   (2014 oil)

"Never heard of 'im."

"That's probably because you're looking at a manhole cover."

Why in my pictures is it always the man making an idiot of himself?

This Birmingham's 'Walk of Fame' began in 2007 and Ozzy Osbourne was its first member.

"Hey man!... that's surreal." "No it's not – it's custard."

▲ **The Custard Factory**   (2011 oil)

"Hey man!… that's surreal." "No it's not – it's custard."

I hadn't really appreciated what a fine frontage this building had until I made this painting. It's a good example of a 19th century factory being converted, in 1992, into modern usage as an arts centre, studios, shops and offices. Alfred Bird (1783-1856) started making powdered custard here at the Devonshire Works factory until the company's relocation in 1964. This picture presented me with probably the one and only good reason I'll ever have to paint custard.

▲ **82 Bus to Bearwood**   (2018 oil)

"Sometimes as a bus driver you just have to grin and bear it."

A bus that goes to Bearwood should have some bears on it surely?

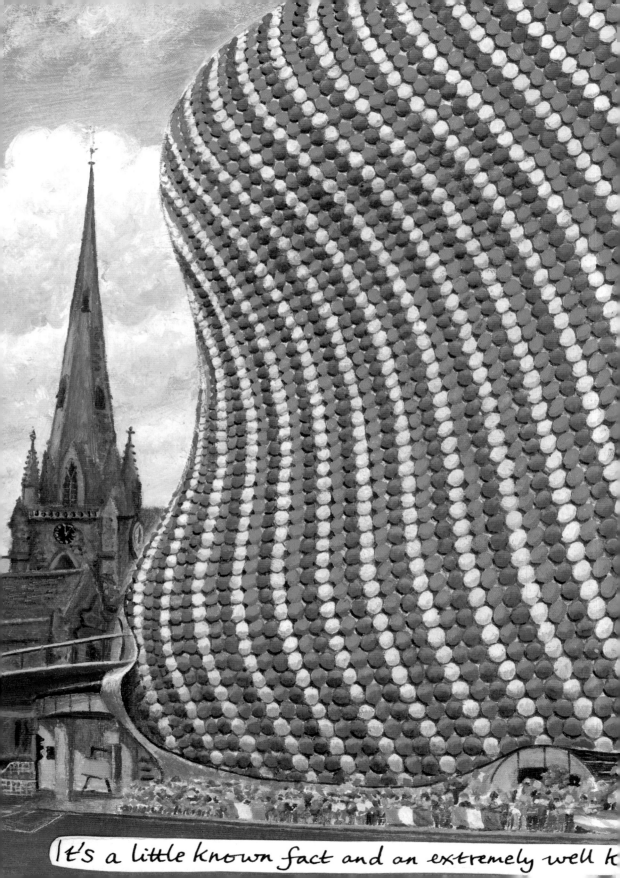

It's a little known fact and an extremely well k

- secret that St Patrick was a Brummie.

These Birmingham cats stay out all night. They're party animals.

www.robspaintings.com

robert.geoghegan@blueyonder.co.uk

robert.geoghegan.5

robertgeogheganart